Man's Basic Instinct

The Inner Enemy of Grace

By
Daniel W. Hill, Ph.D

Copyright © 2017 by Daniel W. Hill, Ph.D.
Tucson, Arizona USA

All Scripture quotations, unless otherwise indicated, are taken from the New American Standard Bible®. Copyright© The Lockman Foundation 1960, 1962, 1963, 1968, 1971, 1972, 1973, 1975, 1977, and 1995. Used by permission (**www.lockman.org**).

All Rights Reserved
Second Printing
ISBN: 978-1981-193226
Create Space: An Amazon Company,
Columbia, SC, USA
2018

Cover art used with permissions:
©Isabel Castaño. www.isabelcastano.com
©Brian Shuster. www.fineartamerica.com

Acknowledgements

I owe a great debt of thanks to my long-time friend Pastor Herman Mattox of Plano, Texas for the spark that ignited this study. He was the first one who introduced me to the idea of man's basic instinct and the unusual illustration found in the epistle of Jude, verse 10. Much of what you will study in this book has been discussed with my friend Herman in the many hours we have spent together in our nearly fifty years of friendship. Thank you, Herman.

Financial Policy

No price is placed on these Bible study materials except for those copies sold through a third-party seller.

We desire to make the study of God's Word available to anyone, regardless of financial ability. God has enriched us with His love, mercy, and grace and we desire to reflect that grace, mercy, and love to others. If you would like to contribute to this ministry, please contact:

Grace Gospel Missions
7739 East Broadway Boulevard
Suite #206
Tucson, Arizona 85710

Phone: (520) 447-9445
E-mail: GGMissions@gmail.com
Website: www.GGMissions.org

TABLE OF CONTENTS

Introduction   1

Chapter One

    Psychology: They sometimes get it Right   7

        Man's Basic Instinct
        Maslow's Pyramid of Needs
        Pavlov's Conditioning
        B.F. Skinner and Operants
        The Carrot and the Stick
        Motivations
        How do We Learn?
        Conditioning and Influences
        Positive Results of Conditioning

Chapter Two

    God: He always gets it Right   29

        What Man says of Man
        What God says of Man
        Grieving the Holy Spirit
        Quenching the Holy Spirit
        The Epistle of Jude
        The Epistles of Paul
        The Story of Job
        David and Solomon
        Isaiah Chapter Twenty-eight
        Summary so Far

Chapter Three

    Man: We can get it Right   61

        Our Education System
        Grace: Always Free
        Karma
        Romans 12:1
        Sowing and Reaping
        Where did this all begin?

Conclusion

    What are we to do?   85

        Denying the Problem
        Finding a Cure
        Living in Grace
        The Problem with Obedience
        Awareness through Prayer

Epilogue   101

Introduction

How many of us struggle with living the Christian life? We probably all understand that we are, as Paul stated in Ephesians 2:8-9, saved *by grace . . . through faith; and that not of yourselves, it is the gift of God; not as a result of works, so that no one may boast.* Yet we turn around and believe we must work or act a certain way to stay saved, to be blessed by God, or to grow in Christ. We make a dramatic shift from grace and faith to law and works. Even the believers who boast most about being in grace will have a performance mentality as their basic understanding of how God deals with them.

Not long ago I attended a *MercyMe* concert. Their lead singer, Bart Millard, spent as much time talking as he did singing. He had a message to tell. After being a Christian for more than thirty years he had discovered what it really meant to live by grace. Most of their latest songs have this as the central message. Bart explained how the church he had been raised in talked about grace but really did not allow grace to permeate every part of their lives. They were still involved in doing, performing, and thinking that through their works God was accepting them more than others. How many of us have fallen for the same lie? I know I did.

I had been a pastor for about twenty years before I ultimately came to an understanding that God not only saved me by grace through faith but now wants me to live before Him in grace through faith. As this became a new reality for me, I began to see the grace message everywhere in the Bible. I began to see the result of grace and faith everywhere in my life. I had to ask myself why it took so long for me to understand the very thing that saved me, God's amazing and matchless grace, also allows me to live the abundant life (John 10:10) with Him now?

As I pondered that question over the last twenty years since my grace awakening, I came to see that there is an inherit part of man's makeup that resists grace. I first learned of this from the Scriptures. Both Jude and Paul talk about the basic instinct of man. I then saw it illustrated in countless stories from the Bible and taught in many passages. However, one of the best lessons about this inherit basic instinct of man did not come from man but from my dog, Abby.

Pat and I have always been more dog people than cat people. The only time we ever had a cat was when we lived in Liberia, West Africa. We were told that a cat was good at keeping away the mice, rats, and cockroaches. We did not really listen to the advice until we saw the first big rat in our house. We then acquired a cat. He was very good at keeping the unwanted critters away. I also very quickly learned, that you cannot train a cat like I had trained my dog.

I had been rather successful at training Abby, our yellow Lab that never turned yellow but stayed as white as snow. When we brought her into our home we determined that she would be well trained. We took her to the Tulsa Kennel Club for puppy classes and then Obedience One and Two. By the time we completed the last class she was *top dog,* a well-trained and loyal pup. One summer I took her to the Texas-Oklahoma youth camp and put her through her paces in front of all the campers. She did the usual things like sit, lie down, speak, and come. After that I really showed her off. I was able to have her sit beside me and without saying a word or giving any hand gesture; she would stay if I started walking on my right foot and follow me if I took off on my left foot. Then I put her at the opposite side of the room and called her to me. When she was half way to me I told her to *stop*, to *lie down*, and after a moment, to *come*. She did exactly as told and she thoroughly enjoyed the applause from the campers.

Whenever anyone saw how obedient Abby was they always asked me, *How did you get her to do that?* It was really not that difficult. A dog will respond to reward and punishment. With Abby it was all reward. The most punishment I ever had to give was just a stern voice. But she loved her treats. Even as a puppy when she did something well, she was rewarded with a treat. When she successfully completed a command, she got a treat. When having difficulty with a command, there would be no treat. She would do about anything to get that little piece of doggy beef jerky. Over time as I gave her fewer treats she still obeyed every command. Soon even a pat on the back or a few kind words telling her that she was a good dog was all she needed.

This was really demonstrated once when we were living up at our Lake Hudson home in Oklahoma. She began to bark to go outside. As I slid open the glass door, she ran out. At that same moment I saw the biggest skunk I had ever seen immediately off the back deck. As Abby tore down the steps I shouted out *noooooooo!* It was almost like something out of a cartoon as she put on the brakes, turned, and then turned and ran up the steps and back inside. Fortunately, Mr. Skunk just wandered off without leaving any scent behind.

As I write this Abby is on her blanket right beside me in my study. She is almost fourteen years old and probably in the last year of her life. I do not ask much of her now, but the little that I do ask she does happily. Abby has been a good dog and a faithful friend.[1]

This wonderful experience with Abby has allowed me to not only understand something about dog nature but also something about human nature. Remember, Abby had been trained with reward and punishment (not much punishment needed). When looking at man's basic instinct we are able to see that it is not that different than the basic instinct of pups. We too respond to reward and punishment. Having learned this from my dog I think I was able to better understand something Jude wrote in his epistle.

> *But these men revile the things which they do not understand; and the things which they know by instinct, like unreasoning animals, by these things they are destroyed* (Jude 10).

---

[1] When I was in Kenya in June of 2017 teaching Pastor's Conferences, Abby died a very peaceful death. We still miss her.

What did Jude[1] mean in stating *by instinct, like unreasoning animals?* We will be examining this concept in this book. How do animals reason? How do we reason? And how does this rob us of the grace life God has for us?

---

[1] We also find a parallel refence to the idea of man's instinct in 2 Peter 2:12. Disagreement prevails as to whether Peter or Jude first wrote of the concept.

Chapter One
Psychology: Sometimes they get it Right

Psychology can be a bad word in the vocabulary and thinking of many conservative, evangelical, Bible-believing Christians. When Psychology takes precedent over biblical teaching the rejection of this field of study is justified. The very word, *psychology*, is taken from two Greek words. The first part of the word, *pysch* or in the Greek *psuche* is defined as the human soul. The second part of the word, *ology,* is from the Greek *logia* and refers to a scientific discipline or study. Put these words together and psychology is the scientific study of the human soul. Yet the secular study of psychology ignores the One Who created the soul. This is like trying to study the Eiffel Tower without any consideration of the man who designed and built it, Gustave Eiffel. If one really wants to understand the soul of man, it would be good to start with the One Who created it.

Man's Basic Instinct

There are times, however, when the secular science of psychology gets it right. They seem to, as does much of secular scientific discovery, stumble upon truth. This is understandable since they are studying something God created. They may not admit that God created the human soul but in their observations of the soul they do see the finger prints of its Creator.

In this study we are going to be looking at man's basic instinct. If you were to do a Google search on *basic instinct*, and after you sorted through the web sites on the Sharon Stone movie, you would come to what psychology has determined to be man's basic instinct. With that search you would find that there is no agreement, even among these secular psychologists and clinicians, as to what is man's basic instinct. Most popular is the idea that *survival* is man's most basic instinct. Yet I have known some precious believers who have lived a full life, like my mother who died at age 99, who had no desire to survive or keep living but only to go on to be with the Lord. When someone knows they have eternal life in Jesus Christ, survival is not that big of a deal.

Another common suggestion offered by psychology as to man's basic instinct is sex. You can read much about how sex is what drives mankind. This too, however, is filled with flaws. The sexual drive in mankind does not begin until puberty and will often lessen in old age. Other secular studies run the gamut on what man's basic instinct might be. These include love, hate, fear, greed, and purpose. Although all these suggestions are found to influence mankind in their actions and attitudes, they are not the underlying instinct of man.

Maslow's Pyramid of Needs

Abraham Maslow in his 1943 study tried looking at all this in a bit of a different way. He sought to answer the question of what man's basic needs are and then attempted to argue backwards to determine basic motives or instinct. He grouped man's needs into six categories: physiological, safety, belonging and love, esteem, self-actualization, and self-transcendence. His conclusion was that these were not just descriptions of man's needs but also stages of needs that develop into what he called a pyramid of needs. His study has been used for decades in every area of training from business to education to government. Many motivational speakers have made a lot of money through seminars and motivational pep talks touting Maslow's pyramid of human needs. Recent attempts to simplify this complex theory of needs and motives have concluded that the three basic needs of humans are drinkable water, nourishing food, and adequate sleep. It is suggested that if you have these you will have a happy life.

Pavlov's Conditioning

Perhaps a better way to come to a conclusion on man's basic instinct is to examine what motivates man. This idea is not unrealized in the secular study of human action. Most psychologists do ponder the question as to man's motivations, but I do not think they seek out the basic or rawest common denominator. Several secular social scientists have come close to understanding what God has said motivates man.

The first was a Russian, Ivan Pavlov, back in the 1890s. We all know about Pavlov's dog. He found that a dog could be trained to respond, by salivating, when a bell would ring. This response was called conditioning. For a period of time, just prior to being given food, a bell would ring. As time went on, when the bell rang, even without food being present to smell, the dog would salivate.

Pavlov and many others since him have used this study to show that man's conditioned response can be manipulated. Their conclusions, simply put, was that we are so conditioned to certain things happening based on what is perceived and expected rather than what really happens that we respond or react prior to the event. A most common illustration of this conditioning is found when we see a person holding a pin near a balloon. We anticipate or are conditioned to expect a boom. So, we wince or cover our ears before the boom even occurs.

I think the most important thing from Pavlov's study and the studies of those who followed him is that we are conditioned. We do much of what we do because we expect there to be a certain outcome from our actions. If you are hungry, you eat food expecting that eating will eliminate your hunger and nourish you. If, however, you ate food that had no nutritional value, you may feel full, but that feeling would be short lived. In a bit more serious example, a person addicted to drugs has been conditioned to think that if he has just one more hit or shot or pill, everything would be fine, but it is not. Thus, how we are conditioned and what our expectations are can be right or wrong, good or evil. Either way, we have been conditioned since early childhood which will play a major role as we explore our basic instinct.

B.F. Skinner and Operants

Another study that sought to determine man's motivation was by Burrhus Frederic Skinner. In the

1920s he felt that the studies of Pavlov, and later John B. Watson and other behaviorists who embraced classical conditioning, were far too simplistic. He believed that the best way to understand behavior was to look at the causes of an action and its consequences. He called this approach *operant conditioning*. Skinner took the previously established idea of the Law of Effect and added a new idea, reinforcement. The idea here is that a behavior that is reinforced will be strengthened and repeated. Just like Pavlov, Skinner, in 1948 used animals in his *Skinner Box* to identify three different factors or what he called *operants* that influence behavior.

> **Neutral operants**: Responses from the environment that neither increase nor decrease the probability of a behavior being repeated.
>
> **Reinforcers**: Responses from the environment that increase the probability of a behavior being repeated. Reinforcers can be either positive or negative.
>
> **Punishers**: Responses from the environment that decrease the likelihood of a behavior being repeated. Punishment weakens behavior.[1]

---

[1] Many online web sites explain in great detail both Pavlov's and Skinner's methods and conclusions. For a brief and concise study of each man and their experiments and finding, Wikipedia does a good job.

Although many of the other conclusions of B.F. Skinner would be rejected by the Bible believing Christian, the fact that he made some great observations on what motivates man to do what man will do is right on the mark.

Perhaps both Pavlov and Skinner happened to get it right especially if we bring both studies together. We are conditioned to do certain behaviors. We do have expectation. When the bell rings we expect food. This was certainly true prior to my lunch hour in high school. As Skinner concluded, we are influenced in our behavior, our expectations, and by what has or has not reinforced that behavior. We learn early on that fire burns and that electricity can be shocking. We also learn that if we do not eat well or sleep well we do not feel good. In our human relationships we also are conditioned to what brings a beneficial response from others.

When moving to West Africa in 2010, I quickly learned that with the Liberians, If you smiled and greeted even a stranger walking past you on the street, you would get a nice smile back. Eventually, I learned a little Liberian English. If I smiled and said *holiday*, which is translated *how is your day*, the response was even greater and the smile bigger. The Liberians like it when Westerners learn their language. The even better payoff was the standard response to *holiday* which is *praise God Oh*. I always loved to hear that. So, there was action, words, a smile on my part, and I expected a specific response. The more I received that response, the more I did the action. If I had done that and received a frown, a hateful look, and was told to *go home white man*, I am sure I would have stopped smiling at people. So, this was a *reinforcer*, to use Skinner's term. That behavior not only increased but soon became a habit.

The Carrot and the Stick

Regardless of how old you are, consider all the things that you have been conditioned to do throughout your lifetime. As Skinner concluded, consider your built-in neutral operants, reinforcers, and punishers. What we do in life is greatly affected by our learned and conditioned behavior.

Often this is called carrot and stick motivation. Examining how this works in a leadership model one web site writer states:

> It's been deeply ingrained in us for the longest time that if we want the people we lead to perform well, we dangle a reward in front of them (carrot) as an incentive, in hope that what's good will be achieved and gets repeated. Likewise, we put up a system of punishment (stick) in its various forms, in hope that what's bad will be avoided and not get repeated. This

is the carrot and stick principle, which is very much *extrinsic* in nature. By whatever name we call it, it's been practiced everywhere: education, workplace, sports, games, family and relationships.[1]

Ray Williams, an executive coach and professional business speaker, has taken this into the world of business with some interesting observations. Again, even secularists get it right sometimes. He looks at all this as part of brain chemistry and cites studies by Hanneke den Ouden and Roshan Cools and their colleagues from the Donders Institute in Nijmegen and New York University[2] that prove that different stimuli will have different results in different people. While the *carrot and stick* work for all mules, it is not as simple with people, or as he is addressing, employees. But in the end the issue is still motivation. People are motivated to do what they do or motivated not to do what they do not do.

This is part of learned behavior or conditioning as good old Pavlov would call it. Skinner would look more at the

---

[1] Coaching Journey, *Carrot and Stick--Intrinsic vs Extrinsic Motivation*, web site: http://coaching-journey.com/carrot-and-stick-intrinsic-extrinsic-motivation/, 2014

[2] Ray Williams, *Wired for Success*, "Carrot and Stick Motivation Revisited by New Research," Web site: https://www.psychologytoday.com/blog/wired-success/201311/carrot-and-stick-motivation-revisited-new-research, 2017.

factors that influence and reinforce behavior. Pavlov, Skinner, and even Williams, see man's actions as a result of what he had learned that is either good for him or bad for him.

Motivations

Even in a casual observation of human behavior one will see that all people of all cultures are motivated by a few very common things. We are motivated by pleasure, profit, and the avoidance of pain. Think of what you are doing right now. You are reading this book. Why? Perhaps you hope to learn something which would be a personal intellectual profit motive. Why did you go to work today? You probably went because of a motive of profit. Would you have gone to work if you knew you would not get paid? And why did you not run that red light on your way home? You probably stopped because you wanted to avoid the pain of a traffic accident of the loss of profit that a traffic ticket would have cost you. Of course, not all pain is financial or physical. Some of the greatest pain we experience in life is emotional. Anyone who has ever endured the hurt of rejection knows well how real that pain is.

For the Christian, God uses these same motivations. What is easiest to see is the profit motive. God promises us blessings in time and reward in eternity. Paul certainly was motivated by reward as he wrote to his protégée in Second Timothy chapter four:

> For I am now ready to be offered, and the time of my departure is at hand. I have fought a good fight, I have finished *my* course, I have kept the faith: Henceforth there is laid up for me a crown of righteousness, which the Lord, the righteous judge, shall give me at that day: and not to me only, but unto all them also that love his appearing (2 Timothy 4:6-8).

We know that if we fulfill the life that God has for us there will be reward in the future.

God also motivates us by pleasure. I hope you really enjoy being a Christian. I hope you enjoy going to church, studying the Word of God, and worshipping God with other like-minded believers. One of the greatest experiences of joy that I can have in life is fellowshipping with other believers. Often this fellowship is at a dinner table enjoying great food. What a pleasure that is! The word *joy* is found more than 160 times in the Bible. Paul's letter to the Philippian church is often called the *Epistle of Joy*. God wants us to have joy and pleasure in the life we live with Him, and that is a powerful motivation.

Last, and I wish it were least, God does use pain. We are His children, and when we move away from Him He holds the option as our Father to discipline us. We should want to avoid the pain of discipline.

When in Liberia I was the spiritual adviser to the 250 Liberian employees at the ELWA[1] mission compound. These men and women worked in the hospital, the school, the radio station, the administration office, and in services. They began each work day with devotions, and over the years there I put together about seven years of daily devotions. I would visit the devotions at times to help the devotion leaders. One morning I heard one of our leaders telling the employees: *if you sin God will punish you*. I stopped him and asked, *what is the punishment for sin?* The entire group quickly answered *death*. I then asked *who was punished for our sins?* You could see the wheels turning in their heads. They finally said *Jesus Christ.* Correct! To make my point, I then said that I love my children, and God loves them as His children. Then for effect I said, *I have never, not ever, not even once, punished my children*. What? Never? were the replies. I smiled and then added, *but there are times I have disciplined them very severely.* They got the point and then I taught how punishment comes from justice, discipline comes from love.

It is because of God's love for us and His desire for us to have His very best that He tells us in Hebrews 12:5-6 . . .

---

[1] ELWA was the call letters for the radio station Sudan Interior Missions started in Monrovia, Liberia in 1952. It stood for *Electronic Liberia West Africa*. Shortly after that the missionaries changed it to *Eternal Love Wins Africa*. Today ELWA is the largest mission compound in the world and includes a hospital, radio station, and school. Pat and I had the privilege of working there with SIM from 2010 to 2015.

My son, do not regard lightly the discipline of the Lord, nor faint when you are reproved by Him, for those whom the Lord loves He disciplines and scourges every son whom He received. God does this because He loves us, and we are motivated not to have Him love us like this. Yes, sometimes God's love hurts. Avoidance of the pain of divine discipline is a legitimate motive in the Christian life. This should keep the Christian in fellowship with God, which means walking by faith in the Holy Spirit.

All mankind, male and female, at any age, in every part of the world, in every culture, is motivated by profit, pleasure, or the avoidance of pain. This is true of the moral man, the immoral man, and the religious man. For the Christian, however, there is one additional motive that God uses that is not available to anyone other than the believer in Christ. That motive is grace. But we will examine more on that in a later chapter.

How do we Learn?

Let us consider how this conditioning (Pavlov) and these influences on our behavior (Skinner) have shaped our lives. We learn very early on in our human existence that if we do good, or things other people consider to be good, we will receive reward. We can go all the way back to potty training. That was something mommy and daddy really wanted you to learn and they influenced and encouraged you in learning that very important human task through praise. You might not remember when you had to learn this but you probably remember standing over the little potty with your own child, sitting there and waiting, and waiting, and waiting. Then when what needed to be done was done, you cheered and applauded and told your little one what a good boy or good girl they were. They soon learned that going on the potty was a good thing and it pleased mommy and daddy. Eventually they did what we all do without the praise and applause. They learned this by getting praise for doing what is good. That is the carrot and that is the way we learned most things in life.

Learning how to behave in this manner continued until eventually it was more like *If you do your chores and keep your grades up, you can use the car on Friday night.* How many of us as children, teenagers, and even young adults have heard a phase from our parents or other adults that began with *If you do . . . then I will do?* You did and not knowing it at the time, you were being conditioned. Your parents had influenced you with *reinforcement operants.*

In the opposite way, you also learned that if you did something that was not good, even bad, you would not get a reward but instead the stick. Many of these *punishment operants*, as Skinner called them, were learned personally. You found that if you hit another child in the sandbox you might be hit back. You learned that eating dirt did not make you feel good. You found out about the dangers all around you, hopefully, before they harmed you. You discovered that fire burns, falling hurts, and eating too much chocolate can give you an upset tummy (although I am still learning that one). You may also have learned some really big life lessons when you found out that you were not to steal, lie, cheat, or harm others.

Back in 1990 Robert Fulghum wrote a book about how everything we learn we really learned in the sandbox or in kindergarten.[1] Consider a partial list of his life lessons learned at an early age:

>Share everything
>Play fair
>Don't hit people
>Put things back where you found them
>Clean up your own mess
>Don't take things that aren't yours
>Say you're sorry when you hurt somebody
>Wash your hands before you eat
>Flush
>Warm cookies and cold milk are good for you
>Take a nap every afternoon

Now how does a child of four or five years old learn these things? They learn by the *carrot and stick* conditioning and neutral, positive, or negative

---

[1] Robert Fulghum, *All I Really Need To Know I Learned In Kindergarten* (New York: Villard Books 1990), page 6-7.

influences. You can trace every behavior or attitude back to discovering that if you do good things there is a reward and if you do bad things there is punishment.

Learning that way does not end with childhood. Once in school we learned that if we study hard we made good grades and there was reward; an A grade or a Gold Star, even praise from teachers and parents. As we progressed through the grades the rewards got bigger. My wife Pat, was given a car at 16, a cute little VW bug, because she earned good grades and did well in school activities. Others go on to receive scholarships because they have good grades. In sports we found that if you worked out, went to practice, and sharpened your skills, you could win the meet or the game and take home a trophy or even better, a scholarship.

For most of us, everything from the potty to our profession was accomplished by finding out that if we did a good job, worked hard, and put in the extra effort, there would be a reward. On the other hand, we also learned that if we slacked off, were lazy, did not put out the effort, and did what was thought not to be good, there would be no reward and there could even be punishment.

Conditioning and Influences

We take the conditioning and the influences that result in positive behavior into our adult lives. In our jobs we know that if we do well we will be rewarded and often we are. We miss work, show up late, do not get the job done and well . . . *your fired!* That is the way life works. In your neighborhood you are a good neighbor, keep your house tidy, your lawn mowed, pick up after your dog, don't play music or the TV too loudly, and others will reward you by being nice to you. Don't do some of those things and the home owner's association (HOA) might try to get rid of you. If we violate certain rules in our townhome we can be fined by HOA. That is the punisher Skinner examined.

Consider one other extremely important area of life, marriage. In marriage husbands and wives quickly learn that if they are nice to their spouse, their spouse will be nice to them. As a good husband I learn what makes my wife happy and feel loved and I am glad to do those things because it will come back in her goodness and love to me. That is just the way relationships work.

Maybe you have suffered through a divorce. As a pastor of 35 years I counseled several couples where all the great biblical advice I could give did not help. The couple divorced and in those few cases where there were children I understood very well why God said in Malachi 2:16a *I hate divorce.* Nothing about it is good.

In the marriage counseling that I did, a few ended in divorce, but many others were helped by the truth and grace of God. The problems I heard of almost always came from expectations that were not met. Many times, I heard the phrase: *He (or she) does not respect me.* Or I heard the indictment: *After all I have done for you.* We have expectations. We are conditioned to think that if we do certain things then we can expect certain things in return. When those expectations are not met, the lack of return becomes a punisher or negative influence on future behavior.

In one of my counseling sessions the wife looked at her husband and complained that he never brought her flowers, he answered by telling her that he did once, fifteen years ago, and she threw them out the next day. He decided then and there he would never do that again. She struggled to remember but then recalled that she did throw them out. She threw them out because her mother was coming to visit that afternoon and her mother had an allergy to cut flowers. Her tears of sorrow came flowing when she realized she never told her husband why she had to remove the flowers from the small apartment.

The carrot and stick life lessons learned over the decades have not always been good lessons. We have learned that if we do bad things then bad things may very well happen to us. Ultimately, we work hard at not breaking any laws, at respecting authorities, and doing the right thing. We know that if we were to live a life of lawlessness we could be jailed or imprisoned. Consider the many men and women who are incarcerated. Somewhere in life they learned incorrectly that if they committed this crime and were to get away with it, everything will not just be good but better. How often have we heard that a person is not sorry for what they did but only sorry of being caught?

Consider how broad this method of learning has been in your life. We eat well, sometimes avoiding foods that taste great, because we know they are not healthy for us. You know that a junk food diet will cause your body harm. That is a punisher, a stick. You also know if you eat good things you will feel good. That is a carrot (and carrots *are* good for you). We learn early on that immorality is not good for us, and that it hurts others even though it may feel good for the moment. We have learned to make judgments of right and wrong because doing that which is wrong can bring about a stick. We do not do the crime because we do not want to do the time. We do not lie because getting caught in a lie hurts.

Think of all the positive enforcers that have shaped your life. The nice things you do because you have learned that when you are nice, others are nice to you. We have learned to be fair and honest because others will be fair and honest with you. Everything from good manners to good morals are learned though positive and negative reinforcers. That is just the way life works and it works pretty well that way.

Paul said in Romans 12:18, *If possible, so far as it depends on you, be at peace with all men.* Paul learned that being at peace with others was a good thing, and he stated he would do all he could to have those peaceful relationships. In our society we live with other people within a framework of governance, economic rules, neighborhoods, workplaces, schools, and families. Striving for peace with all men, we draw on the lessons learned from childhood: Rewarded for the good and punished for the bad. The reward may not be a trophy or a pay raise or a ticker-tape parade. It may be a simple smile or a kind word that will reinforce more good behavior. The punishment may not be years in prisons or heavy fines but a rejection of not being invited to a party or of people not wanting to associate with you. That is the way the world works.

Positive Results of Conditioning

I do not want you to think that I am being critical about the behavior exhibited as a result of this learned carrot and stick behavior. I am not. I would not want to live in a world where others had no interest in doing good to be rewarded and not accepting that if they did bad there would be some sort of punishment. We exist in our polite, most of the time, fair, decent, and harmonious society because of our conditioning and influences. Without that we would at best have a rude society and at worse, have anarchy.

In the Old Testament book of Proverbs there is great wisdom. The wisdom, however, is not just for the believer; it is wisdom for all mankind. Many of the passages speak directly to the one who has a personal faith relationship with God, but a majority of the passages are good advice for all mankind. Both believers and unbelievers, according to Proverbs, live well in society by hard work, honesty, good manners, and morals. Proverbs has a lot of carrot and stick verses since this is the way the world works. Consider Proverbs 6: 6-11

> Go to the ant, O sluggard, Observe her ways and be wise, Which, having no chief, Officer or ruler, Prepares her food in the summer *And* gathers her provision in the harvest. How long will you lie down, O sluggard? When will you arise from your sleep? A little sleep, a little slumber, A little folding of the hands to rest-- Your poverty will come in like a vagabond And your need like an armed man.

God is telling us that being a sluggard, who is a lazy person, will result in poverty.

Nearly twenty times in Proverbs we find the *if . . . then* grammatical construction. These are telling the reader that if he or she does something, something will result. Sometimes these are positive reinforcers and at other times negative reinforcers. Our God Who created us knows how we tick. God knows that in our world, the world He created, and we are traveling through, that mankind, especially unbelieving mankind, needs to live knowing that there is reward for good and punishment for evil. If man does not recognize this, then orderly society falls apart.

In the end, there is nothing wrong with the fact that we live in a structured society. We go to school, we work, and we have relationships with family and community. We know that for the most part if we do good, good things will come back to us and that if we do bad things bad things will come back to us.

Let us go back to the question we had at the beginning of this chapter, *what is man's basic instinct?* What is a part of man's very motivation in life that is a part of him from birth to death?

> The basic instinct of man is his learned understanding that doing good will bring reward and doing evil will bring punishment and his behavior that results from that understanding.

We have seen what psychology, which sometimes gets it right, has said about this. Now we need to see what God in His Word says about man's basic instinct.

Chapter Two
God: He always gets it Right

When Pat and I lived in Liberia we each taught one course every semester at Monrovia Bible College. They gave me the position of Visiting Professor of New Testament Studies. We did not get paid, but the title looks really good on my resume. The first class I taught was New Testament Survey to about sixty students. When the time came for me to give the first test, I opened in prayer, then went down the center aisle handing out the exam. Walking back to the front of the class I turned around and saw about forty students looking at each other's papers and copying answers they thought more correct than theirs. There was no attempt to hide what they were doing I loudly said, *What are you doing? You are Christians. You are in a Bible College. You are in a Bible Class. You are taking a Bible test. AND YOU ARE CHEATING!* One of the young men spoke up and said: *Oh No, Doc, we are not cheating; we are just helping each other.* For me that was a good illustration that even the best of young men and women are not inherently good. Given a chance, they would cheat and then excuse or deny the sin by calling it something else.

What Man Says of Man

In both secular and theological disciplines, the study of man is called Anthropology. One of the secular definitions is: *the study of human biological and physiological characteristics and their evolution.* Merrian-Webster gives the theological definition of the word as: *dealing with the origin, nature, and destiny of human beings.* We have seen examples of what the secular science of psychology has to say about man but for our study it is more important to examine what God has to say. After all, if we believe that God created us, it would stand to reason to listen to what our Creator has to say about His creation. A stark difference in the way secularism views man's nature and what God say about man's nature is that man sees man as basically good and God does not.

Ray Comfort, in an online blog in 2014, summed up the secular view very well when he wrote:

Humanism says that man is basically good, and that when he does something morally wrong, some outside influence has caused him to go off the rails--such as not having a father figure, poverty, bad friends, etc.

Dr. Christopher L. Heffner, a leading American psychologist who embraces humanism, in a web article defends the idea that people are basically good:

> Humanistic Psychology gets its name from its belief in the basic goodness and respect of humankind. Its roots are based in existential psychology or the understanding and acceptance of one's own existence and responsibility . . . The individual, merely by being human, possess an inherent worth. Actions may not be positive, but this does not negate the value of the person.

What God Says of Man

Man thinks that man is basically good. Although that sounds a bit self-serving and self-defending, we should not be surprised. God, however, gives us a completely different take on those He created. Consider these few passages:

> **Jeremiah 17:9** *The heart is more deceitful than all else And is desperately sick; Who can understand it?*

Romans 7:18 *For I know that nothing good dwells in me, that is, in my flesh; for the willing is present in me, but the doing of the good is not.*

Romans 3:10 *There is none righteous, not even one.*

Isaiah 64:6 *For all of us have become like one who is unclean, And all our righteous deeds are like a filthy garment; And all of us wither like a leaf, And our iniquities, like the wind, take us away.*

There is a great divide between what man thinks of himself and what God declares man to be. Since the Fall God has made a distinction in the human race. This distinction is between those who are in darkness and those, who by grace through faith, were moved into the light. God sees the entire human race in two camps, those who have believed in His Son as their Savior and those who have not. Of fallen man God has some very strong things to say. Consider these ten descriptive words that are used in the New Testament Epistles by Paul to describe the fallen state of man's thinking:

Depraved Mind	Romans 1:28
Hardened	2 Corinthians 3:14
Blinded	2 Corinthians 4:4
Futile	Ephesians 4:17
Darkened	Ephesians 4:18
Hostile	Colossians 1:21
Deceived	Colossians 2:8

Fleshly	Colossians 2:18
Depraved	2 Timothy 3:8
Defiled	Titus 1:15

Consider also what God says of man's fallen condition:

No concern for the thoughts of God, Romans 1:25

Blinded by Satan, 2 Corinthians 4:4

Not wise but foolish, Psalm 14:1

Dead in sin, Romans 8:5-8

Affections set on things of the earth, Colossians 3:2

Walks in darkness, John 12:35-36

Faces eternal damnation, 2 Thessalonians 1:9

Living in the flesh and not in the Spirit, Romans 8:1-5

These two lists paint a pretty bleak picture of God's estimation of unbelieving man. But we who have put our faith alone in Christ alone for the forgiveness of sins and for the receiving of eternal life know that when we made that faith decision, all things became new. In 2 Corinthians 5:17 we are told, *Therefore if anyone is in Christ, he is a new creature; the old things passed away; behold, new things have come.* For as much as God says

about fallen man He has even more to say about the wonderful position we now have in Christ.

Grieving the Holy Spirit

We all know, however, that we can choose to sin. We sin in our thoughts, words, and deeds. When the believer sins he grieves the Holy Spirit (Ephesians 4:30). There is not a great upside to sin. In Africa, when I teach on eternal security, there is always someone who says, *well you are telling us that we can just go out and sin all we want and still go to heaven.* I usually begin by telling them that they do not need me to tell them to sin; they do that pretty well on their own. I then explain that there is not much advantage to letting sin run rampant in their life. When we sin, we break fellowship with God, and if our sin involves others we break fellowship with them. If you are known as a liar, a thief, a gossip, a slanderer, or a cheat, others just will not want to be around you. Some sins can result in criminal charges and put you behind bars. Other sins, such as sexual immorality, can cause physical ailment and diseases. We also open ourselves up to divine discipline. When we chose to sin or continue in sin, we reject the love that our heavenly Father has for us.

Sin in the believer's life can be the result of fear, anger, and shame. These are hidden lifestyles that we carry with us as part of the old man and can manifest itself in a great deal of dysfunction in relationships with others.

A believer trapped in a lifestyle of fear will avoid others, not seek relationships, or be afraid to join with others even in a church. Anger can do the same thing.

We occasionally hear of a person who has *snapped*. That happens when anger boils up to a breaking point. Shame is also a cruel master. Some believers have such a great shame that they think God can never forgive them or use them.

These lifestyles when manifested socially are unacceptable. Rather than admit sin and seek the power of the Holy Spirit to be conformed to Christ, the believer will cover up these lifestyles. The common cover-ups to lifestyle sins are denial, pretense, demanding, and self-protection. Some Christians have become very adept at using these cover-ups and will appear to others to be very spiritual. In reading the Gospels I find that the Pharisees who were in a lot of fear and anger, were very good at using pretense and demanding to hide their lifestyle of sin. They appear to be very holy, but Jesus calls it a pretense.

Quenching the Holy Spirit

There is, however, something more subtle than sin, more subtle than even hidden lifestyles of sin. That is our nature, not just our sin nature but our old nature, the old self. It is the old man who is conditioned just like Pavlov's dog and influenced by operants just like Skinner described which is still with us after salvation.

While in practice the Christian may choose to go back to some of those attitudes and actions of fallen man, in position he is a new creature in Christ. The fact that we can, by our free will, chose to go back to what the Bible calls the *Old Man* is why we are challenged in Colossians 3:9 and Ephesians 4:22 to put off the *Old Man and put on the New Man.*

We have all heard the saying, *old habits are hard to break.* Most of us have more than just heard it, we have lived through it. I did not become a Christian until I was twenty years old. Through my unbelieving teenage years, a short time on active duty with the US Navy Reserves, and in my first year of college, I had picked up a lot of habits. Not all of them were bad habits. My dad who was from the south instilled in me manners, and that became a good habit. There were, however, some bad habits, not only in actions but also in thinking. My mother was a worrier. She could over-think even the smallest of things. I find that I can too. I am sure I have claimed the promise of Philippians 4:6, *Be anxious for nothing, but in everything by prayer and supplication with thanksgiving let your requests be made known to God* at least a million times. Even now, after being saved for over fifty years, I do fall into worry. But now I call it being *overly concerned* (I am being facetious)

Satan worked very hard to keep you from being saved. If you have believed in Christ, Satan failed. Now he will work just as hard at keeping you out of fellowship with God. The Bible calls this being carnal, walking indarkness, walking in the flesh, temporal spiritual death, being asleep, and grieving or quenching the Holy Spirit. Being out of fellowship is an absolute position just as sure as being in fellowship with God is an absolute position. We are at any time either spiritual or carnal. In Ephesians 5:14 Paul wrote of the believer as either being awake or asleep, alive or dead, in darkness or light. These are not relative but absolute positions for the believer.

If Satan cannot tempt us into sin, and remember we sin in thought, word, and deed, he will try to involve us in works that are apart from the power of the Spirit of God. He perhaps has found that this method of derailing the child of God to be more successful than sin. In the end, as Paul observed, *whatever is not of faith is sin* (Romans 14:23). We have already seen that sin does not have many advantages and it is also rather apparent. If we are to be honest, we know when we sin and if not, others are sure to tell us.

Works, legalism, and law however, are much more subtle. If Satan can get the believer into works, thinking that he is spiritual by what he is doing rather than who he is in Christ, he has gotten the believer out of fellowship. Getting out of fellowship through legalism is called, in 1 Thessalonians 5:19, *quenching* the Spirit. When you quench a fire, you put out the flame, the power of the fire. When we quench the Holy Spirit we put out the power that God has for us. Satan has been so successful at this approach that he has been able to cause some believers to be out of fellowship for a life time. One reason he is so successful with this approach is because of man's basic instinct.

Here is the point. Just because we are saved does not mean that all of our old thinking vanishes. That is especially true of our basic instinct. That basic instinct that we have had ever since infancy, that we used to have success in family, school, work, and society, is something still being carried with us. That basic instinct mentioned by Jude, Peter, and Paul is illustrated in the thinking and actions of men and women throughout the Bible.

The Epistle of Jude

In Jude 10 we read, *But these men revile the things which they do not understand; and the things which they know by instinct, like unreasoning animals, by these things they are destroyed.*

The Epistle of Jude is one of the more interesting letters in the New Testament. The first thing noted is what makes this short letter unusual. Jude had intended to write a salvation tract but was compelled by the Holy Spirit to write a defense of the faith. This letter is also unusual in that, although it is only twenty-five verses in the English text, at least half the verses are illustrations either from the Old Testament, nature, or future things.

The language is some of the most colorful and illustrative found in the New Testament. In verse 10 Jude is warning about the apostates of his day. He tells us they revile, or better, blaspheme (to speak evil of) things they do not understand. Not only do they not understand or comprehend, but they do not even have a knowledge of them. What they do not understand or know (found in verse 8) includes any authority even of angelic authorities. They have no comprehension of things above them in either the spiritual realm or in the realm of authorities.

So, with this lack of understanding and knowledge, they blaspheme, speak evil. It is interesting how this is so common to man. When we do not understand something, we suppress it and end up speaking against it. The Gnostics of Jude's day boasted in their superior knowledge. He says they do not have superior knowledge, but rather an inferior knowledge. They do not understand what is above them and only know what is below them like animals. Such reasoning is not on things above but on things below. What they do know is by *instinct, like unreasoning animals.* How do animals reason? By the carrot and the stick. Remember my dog, Abby, and how she learned by reward and punishment? This falls in line with Pavlov's dog and the influences of Skinner's operants. This manner of learning, however, is not limited to animals. We have already seen how all of us function in this basic instinct from birth to death.

The English Standard Version translates this phase as: *like unreasoning animals, understand instinctively.* In a parallel passage in 2 Peter 2:12 the Apostle writes: *But these, like unreasoning animals, born as creatures of instinct to be captured and killed, reviling where they have no knowledge, will in the destruction of those creatures also be destroyed.* Both of these usages look at the instinct of animals, being conditioned and influenced by reward and punishment, and apply that characteristic to man. We are creatures of instinct. We do not reason out every action or every thought with some mental process of weighing the pros and cons, truth and fiction. We most often just act because this is our basic instinct and we have learned that if we do certain things we will receive certain things back. Smile and others smile back, speak a kind word and receive a kind word in return. Work hard and earn a raise. Study hard and receive a good grade. We have been conditioned to expect that when we do good things we will be rewarded, and when we do bad things we will be punished. That does not take reason; we do this by instinct just like animals. As has been discussed, that is not a bad thing; we move along in society rather well by using that which we have been conditioned to do.

The Epistles of Paul

The Apostle Paul looked at this basic instinct in a different way. He was not dealing with apostates who blaspheme spiritual things but with legalism. Legalism can manifest itself in the life of the Christian in a number of ways. Paul was writing in Colossians Chapter Two about a type of legalism that thinks that one is approved by God because of what he does or does not do. This is most often comparative in that one compares himself with other in his performance. This was the legalism of the Pharisees who thought God was really impressed by how they dressed, spoke, acted, and all they did and did not do.

There is no better illustration of this than the one Jesus gave when He spoke of the Pharisee and the tax collector in Luke 18:9-14,

> Two men went up into the temple to pray, one a Pharisee, and the other a tax-gatherer. The Pharisee stood and was praying thus to himself, God, I thank Thee that I am not like other people: swindlers, unjust, adulterers, or even like this tax-gatherer. I fast twice a week; I pay tithes of all that I get. But the tax-gatherer, standing some distance

away, was even unwilling to lift up his eyes to heaven, but was beating his breast, saying, God, be merciful to me, the sinner! I tell you, this man went down to his house justified rather than the other; for everyone who exalts himself shall be humbled, but he who humbles himself shall be exalted.

We have the Pharisees with us today who are quick to boast of their spiritual performance and what they think makes them special to God.

The second form of legalism that relates directly to what Paul first wrote of in Galatians, expanded on in Romans, and then addressed in Colossians is a legalism that thinks that God will only bless you if you obey all the rules. This legalism is based on a formula of law and works rather than grace and faith.

In Colossians Chapter 2:8 and 20, Paul twice used the phrase, the *elementary principles of the world.* In Colossians 2:8 he writes,

> See to it that no one takes you captive through philosophy and empty deception, according to the tradition of men, according to the elementary principles of the world, rather than according to Christ.

The first thing that should grab our attention in verse 8 is that these elementary principles are according to philosophy and empty deception. Furthermore, they are according to traditions or rules of men rather than according to Christ. Then in verses 20 and 21 Paul gives us an explanation of these elementary principles. He writes that it is living in the world and freely submitting to decrees or set rules. We know that the Jews of Paul's day had a lot of rules that they had added to the 613 laws of Moses. He then describes these rules as: *do not handle, do not taste, do not touch.*

In these verses Paul describes how totally empty this legalism is. Colossians 2:20-23 states:

> If you have died with Christ to the elementary principles of the world, why, as if you were living in the world, do you submit yourself to decrees, such as, Do not handle, do not taste, do not touch! (which all refer to things destined to perish with use) -- in accordance with the Commandments and teachings of men? These are matters which have, to be sure, the appearance of wisdom in self-made religion and self-abasement and severe treatment of the body, but are of no value against fleshly indulgence.

Paul would be hard pressed to speak of the activities of legalism any less favorably. They are destined to perish with use (they do not work), are from man, have the appearance of wisdom, constitute self-made religion, and are of no value against sins of the flesh. Yet these are the types of things that religious people or even religious performance thinking Christians engage in. If you were to ask most Christians what being a Christian is all about, they would most likely explain that it is about being good. Others may add that it means keeping the Ten Commandments. Ask most people if they know they are going to heaven and the answer often will be only if they are good enough.

In West Africa people use words and quotes from the Bible as good luck talisman. When opening a business, it is good luck to give it a Bible name. I remember in Ghana seeing the Sampson and Delilah Beauty Parlor and Barbering Shop. Many taxicabs have the name of God or a Bible word painted across the back window. When in such a taxi I would tell the driver that I noticed what he had on his back window and then ask if he were a Christian? The answer was always *yes*. I would then ask if he was going to heaven? and that question invoked more hesitancy and *I hope so* as the answer. At that point I would ask him: suppose you died today, right now, we were hit by a truck and we both died, and we go to heaven, and God asks *why should I let you in?* What would you tell God? I could write a book on the answers to that question, but usually the answers would revolve around being good enough. Some would say they try to keep the Ten Commandments, they try to go church every Sunday, they are good to their family, and on and on.[1] We should not be surprised at these answers. We will not be surprised if we remember how man is wired, how he is conditioned. If I do good I will be rewarded, but if I do bad I will be punished.

In Romans Chapter Two Paul tells us that this basic instinct is an ingrained part of the human soul. He is talking about the Gentiles who have no background in a relationship with God as do the Jews. Gentiles do not have the Mosaic Law, but even with that, he states in Romans 2:14-15:

> For when Gentiles who do not have the Law do instinctively the things of the Law, these, not having the Law, are a law to themselves, in that they show the work of the Law written in their hearts, their conscience bearing witness and their thoughts alternately accusing or else defending them.

How does the non-believing man know there are things that are good to do and things that are bad to do? They have a law to themselves and it is written in their hearts. Their conscience, the part of the soul that establishes our norms and standards, is an instinctive part of their thoughts. This verse shows that the basic instinct is an

---

[1] Of course, I would use these opportunities to witness to them and tell them about the grace of salvation by faith the finished work of Jesus Christ on the Cross.

inherit part of man. Inherently man has found that there are things that are good and things that are bad. This becomes a part of his instinctive nature. He is so sure of these standards that he will defend himself regarding what he does or accuse (or excuse) himself of his wrong doing. This verse shows us that even the unbeliever has what some may call a moral compass. This conditioned moral compass results in his doing good to be rewarded and knowing that if he does bad he may very likely be punished.

As we have noted, this is not a bad thing when it comes to our living among others and striving to do well in the family, at school, or work. It is also good to know that there are those things we should not do, and if we persist in doing them, there will be ramifications and even punishment. That is the way the world works. That is how we survive as social beings. But that is also a great problem when it comes to our intimacy with God through Jesus Christ and in grace and the power of the Holy Spirit.

God tells us in Isaiah 55:8-9 *For My thoughts are not your thoughts, Nor are your ways My ways, declares the LORD. For as the heavens are higher than the earth, So are My ways higher than your ways And My thoughts than your thoughts.* God's thoughts, God's ways are not man's thoughts or ways. His thoughts and His ways are higher, much higher than ours. Man often forgets that God created him in His image. It is not man creating God in his fallen image. Yet that is exactly what most of mankind does. When you study non-Christian religions of the world, you learn that their god or gods are more like men than gods. Man has to work really hard at pleasing his pagan god. Man has to offer great sacrifices to invoke the mercy or blessings of his god. But our God's ways are not man's ways.

The Story of Job

We all know about the story of Job. He was suffering greatly and yet he would not deny God. His children all died, his wealth was gone, his wife abandoned him, and he ended up covered with open sores sitting on the sterile field of an ash heap. It was then that his friends came. These three men were friends and they sincerely wanted to help. For seven days they sat with Job not speaking. When they did speak, however, their words were not from the Lord but from their basic instinct. When Eliphaz finally speaks he tells Job in Job 4:7, *Remember now, whoever perished being innocent? Or where were the upright destroyed?* In other words, if you were really upright you would not be suffering. For the next ten chapters Job's friends try to convince him that at some time he must have done some great sin that is now causing this great punishment. Job clings tightly to his self-righteousness, but allows it to spill over into self-pity and then arrogance. In chapter twenty-nine he begins to boast of his onetime greatness. His friends continue to give counsel, but although much of what they say is true, it is tainted with that which is false. We know that it only takes a little leaven to leaven the whole loaf.

Job would not take the bait offered by his comforters. He would not admit that he was suffering because of some secret sin. By the time we come to Chapter thirty-two his friends give up. Job 32:1 tells us, *Then these three men ceased answering Job, because he was righteous in his own eyes.* It is then that we find that all this time there had been a fourth comforter quietly sitting by.

In Job Chapter Thirty-Two Elihu begins to speak. Of all the powerful things this man has to say one of the most memorable is in found in Job 35:4-8 as he answers Job:

> I will answer you, And your friends with you. Look at the heavens and see; And behold the clouds--they are higher than you. If you have sinned, what do you accomplish against Him? And if your transgressions are many, what do you do to Him? If you are righteous, what do you give to Him, Or what does He receive from your hand? Your wickedness is for a man like yourself, And your righteousness is for a son of man.

Elihu understood that God's thoughts were not man's thoughts and that God's ways were not man's ways. He knew that man's good deeds or bad deeds added nothing to God and they took nothing away from God.

Elihu had learned something that we all must learn: God is God and we are not. And since He is God, our basic instinct or thinking that has been so conditioned by our life with men, does not count in our life with God. The story of Job illustrates man's basic instinct and how it does not work with God.

David and Solomon

We can also see the problem of man's basic instinct in trying to relate to God in the life of Solomon as it is compared to the life of his father, David. David, although a man of great sin (murder and adultery), is called both in the Old Testament and the New, a man after God's own heart (1 Samuel 13:14 and Acts 13:22). Long after David died the success of his ruling descendants was measured by whether or not they walked in the ways of their father David. David left a strong United Kingdom of God's people for his son Solomon to rule.

Solomon's life never measured up to that of his father. In 1 Kings 11:6 we are even told that, *Solomon did what was evil in the sight of the LORD, and did not follow the LORD fully, as David his father had done.* When Solomon died in 930 BC the kingdom that his father David had built was divided into two nations. Both father and son, David and Solomon, were kings over a united Israel. Both ruled for forty years from Jerusalem. They were alike in many worldly ways but very different in their relationship to the one true God of Israel. David was a man of grace and faith and knew that his righteousness added nothing to God, and his sin took nothing away from God. David knew he was at the mercy and grace of God. Solomon never quite learned that lesson.

Perhaps no place is this better illustrated than when both kings did something that was very similar. David offered a prayer in 1 Chronicles 16:8-36 when he brought the Ark of the Covenant into the Tabernacle. In 1 Kings 8:12-61 Solomon also offered a prayer forty years later when he brought the Ark of the Covenant into the newly built Temple. Two kings, two prayers, both having to do with the Ark of the Covenant, yet two very different prayers.

A simple reading of the two prayers shows that David filled his prayer with the great things God had done for his people. Solomon's prayer was filled with all the things he thought were great that he had done for God. When David wanted to speak of the covenant God had made with His people he said in 1 Chronicles 16:15-16:

> Remember His covenant forever, The word which He commanded to a thousand generations, The covenant which He made with Abraham, And His oath to Isaac.

When Solomon wanted to talk about the covenant God had made with Israel he said in I Kings 8:56:

Blessed be the LORD, who has given rest to His people Israel, according to all that He promised; not one word has failed of all His good promise, which He promised through Moses His servant.

David was calling upon the people to remember the covenant God made with Abraham because it was an unconditional covenant of grace. Solomon called upon God to remember the conditional covenant of blessing and cursing He made with the whole nation of Israel through Moses.[1] Solomon was impressed with the works he had done for God, and he expected God to be impressed with him. This is basic instinct thinking.

The response of the people to the prayers of these two kings is also very telling. When David concluded his prayer, we are told in 1 Chronicles 16:36 that, *all the people said, Amen, and praised the LORD.* At the end of Solomon's prayer, we are told in I Kings 8:66 that as the people left, *they blessed the king.* If people are blessing the Lord, it is the Lord who is getting the praise. If people are blessing the king, it is the king who is getting the praise.

We might wonder why God chose to give us so much information in the Bible about David and Solomon.

---

[1] The Mosaic Covenant or the Mosaic Law was never given as a way of salvation or sanctification for God's people. It was given to be the law of a nation and was a required by all people in that nation alone, believers, unbelievers, and even travelers in the land.

Perhaps it is because God wanted us to see the difference between two men of very equal status and background and yet, how one lived by grace and the other lived by his basic instinct.

Isaiah Chapter Twenty-Eight

Isaiah 28:8-13 is one of the most often quoted Bible passages and yet most often misunderstood. In the context God is speaking through the prophet Isaiah to the Northern Kingdom of Israel that is about to fall to the Assyrians.[1] As he is speaking this woe against them, God also gives a warning to the people of Judah.

A rhetorical question is asked and answered in verse 9 which asks to whom will God teach knowledge and interpret the message? The answer is given prophetically to be little children. I am reminded of John 1:12 *But as many as received Him, to them He gave the right to become children of God, even to those who believe in His name.* The ones who are the children, the ones who will believe in His name, are perhaps the Gentile believers. They will listen as Israel rejects their Messiah.

Verse 10 is a bit difficult because the NASV adds the words *He says*. This addition is not found in other translations and is not in the Hebrew text. The statement

---

[1] This happened in 722 BC as the Assyrian army under the leadership of Sargon II destroyed Samaria,

of verse 10 is not something God is saying but what is being said by those who are not receiving the knowledge God's teaching or the message He is giving. The New International Version (NIV) seems to come closest to the original intent when it translates verse 10 as:

> Do and do, do and do,
> rule on rule, rule on rule,
> a little here, a little there.

The next verse begins with the word, *Very well then*. So, if the ones who are not learning or listening decide instead to do works and keep rules and take just a little here and there from God's Word, God will use those who have stammering lips and a foreign tongue. We should recall the objection to the Apostle preaching on the Day of a Pentecost when they did preach in foreign tongues and were accused of being drunk (Acts 2:11-13).

In Isaiah 28:12 we have what God offers to His Old Testament people. *Here is rest, give rest to the weary, And, Here is repose.* God offers rest to the believer. The first *rest* is a Hebrew word for *a place of rest*. The second word *rest* means to *settle down into rest*. The word *repose* means to really settle into a good long comfortable rest. One thing about resting is that when resting you are not working. In verse 10 the people wanted to do a lot of doing. God instead offers rest from their doing. Rest in the Bible comes because work is finished. God rested on the seventh day because His work was finished. God has finished the work for us in Jesus Christ and although historically that had not happened back in Isaiah's day, it was a sure promise of God that the people could depend on. To depend on the work of God takes faith. Rest in the Bible for man always comes from faith. So, God is calling His people to stop their works and keeping of rules and rest in faith. But then we have what might be the saddest words in the Bible. Verse 12 ends with, *but they would not listen.*

They rejected. They did not even listen to the offer to cease from their works and rest in God's finished work by faith. But that should not surprise us. The basic instinct of man has him believing that if he does good, does a lot of doing and following of rules, he will receive benefit and blessing.

If the last words of verse 12 are the saddest in the Bible, the first words of verse 13 may be the most frightening. *So the word of the Lord will be to them . . .* When they go to the Word they are not going to see grace, they are not going to find rest. Instead, they will find what they have predetermined to seek, *Do and do, do and do, rule on rule, rule on rule.* They will establish their laws, and rules, and legalism by only taking from the *Bible a little here, a little there.*

Keil and Delitzsch Commentary on the Old Testament states of verse 13:

> Their policy was a very different one from being still, or believing and waiting *[resting by faith]*. And therefore the word of Jehovah, which they regarded as an endless series of trivial commands, would be turned in their case into an endless series of painful sufferings. To those who thought themselves so free, and lived so free, it would become a stone on which they would go to pieces, a net in which they would be snared, a trap in which they would be caught.[1] *[Brackets and Italics mine]*

God will allow them to do just that. Realize that the same Bible in which you find the love, mercy, and grace of God is where the legalist finds his works, laws, and rules. If you come to the Bible having rejected grace, having rejected faith as the only way to honor God, you will find just about anything you might want to find. This is what Jesus warned of in Mark 4:23-24.

> If anyone has ears to hear, let him hear . . . Take care what you listen to. By your standard of

---

[1] Karl Fredreich Keil and Franz Delitzsch, *Commentary on the Old Testament,* translated from the German by James Martin (Peabody, MA: Hendrickson Publishers, 1996) Vol. 7, Isaiah 28.

measure, it will be measured to you; and more will be given you besides.

We all have ears but are they the ears of grace or the ears of law? The standard will either be one of law and works or grace and faith. If the latter is rejected, as it was by the people of Isaiah 28:12, then the Bible will become to them nothing more than a book of rules without relationship.

Why would God do this? Why would God allow people to so misuse His Word? The answer is given in the last part of Isaiah 28:13. *That they may go and stumble backward, be broken, snared and taken captive.* God has what we might call an end game. He knows what Warren Wiersbe was fond of saying, *works do not work!* God wants the legalist to go for his legalism and in the end, stumble, be broken, snared, taken captive and hopefully, see that the only way up is by receiving grace through faith. I have known too many Christians who have abandoned the Christian life because they thought it to be too hard. They, however, were the ones making it hard by their legalism. Whenever anyone has complained to me that the Christian life was a life hard to live, I tell them they are doing something wrong. My Lord said in Matthew 11:28 and 30, *Come to Me, all who are weary and heavy-laden, and I will give you rest . . . For My yoke is easy and My burden is light.*

Later in Isaiah 28, as God is describing the boastfulness of these who reject what God offers of grace, He states in verse 16, *Behold, I am laying in Zion a stone, a tested stone, A costly cornerstone for the foundation, firmly placed. He who believes in it will not be disturbed.* The greatest extent of God's grace was in the sending of His Son to earth to be our Savior. He is the rock, the stone, the corner stone. Jesus, the highest expression of grace, was stumbled over by the ones who sought righteousness by law. Paul refers to them in Romans 9:30-33:

> What shall we say then? That Gentiles, who did not pursue righteousness, attained righteousness, even the righteousness which is by faith; but Israel, pursuing a law of righteousness, did not arrive at that law. Why? Because they did not pursue it by faith, but as though it were by works. They stumbled over the stumbling stone, just as it is written, BEHOLD, I LAY IN ZION A STONE OF STUMBLING AND A ROCK OF OFFENSE, AND HE WHO BELIEVES IN HIM WILL NOT BE DISAPPOINTED.

These people in Paul's day had the same mind as the ones in Isaiah's day. They rejected the *rest* that God offered though faith and instead sought a righteousness by works. Why? Because they believed that if they did good they would be rewarded. Their basic instinct was keeping them from what God wanted them to have.

Summary so Far

We have seen that psychologist, even when they study man without any consideration of the creator, does make some accurate observations. There are those like Pavlov and Skinner who see the character and actions of man as a product of conditioning and influences. Psychology tells that we are reinforced to do those things for which we derive some benefit. It also tells us that we avoid doing those things for which we have received some punishment or negative benefit.

As we apply these simple observations to man we see that this is the way man works. This benefit or punishment cycle, sometimes called the carrot and stick, has taught man how to behave and how to succeed in society. Study hard, work hard, be kind, do not break laws, treat others as you would want them to treat you, and you will have a happy life. We developed this basic instinct from our very early childhood and it continues to be reinforced long into adulthood. It is ingrained into the thinking of all men that if they do good there will be reward and if they do things that are bad there will be punishment. This is the basic instinct of man.

God does not dismiss this basic instinct as being bad for mankind. The book of Proverbs and many other passages tell man how to get along with others in society by means of his basic instinct. We can be very glad that most people on planet earth have learned by way of their basic instinct to strive to do good, to desire to do that which brings benefit to themselves and to others. We can also be glad that most people want to avoid doing things that are bad that will lead to problem and even punishment. It is this basic instinct that makes the world go 'round so to speak. The problem comes when we try to use this basic instinct that is so much a part of us in our relationship with God.

God is a God of grace and while the basic instinct tells us to do good things to earn what we deserve, God says grace gives us what we do not earn or deserve. Here is where the problem comes in. Man has been conditioned through his lifetime to earn and deserve. He has been influenced by various positive and negative operants or reinforcers to think that to receive good he must do good. If he receives punishment it is because it because of what he did that was not good. This basic instinct thinking has served man well in the world as he lives in society. This basic instinct thinking has worked as he has grown to adulthood, in school, marriage, work, and in the community. But then he comes to his new relationship with God through faith in Jesus Christ. This new relationship begins with salvation which is by grace through faith; it is not of works (Ephesians 2:8-9). There is no boasting. In mercy God has not given man what man deserves, and in grace God gives man what he has not earned or deserved.

This is so contrary to man's basic instinct that he has a hard time accepting grace. In the next chapter we are going to see just how difficult accepting grace is and then consider where the basic instinct came from. We will conclude this study by looking at how we can overcome our basic instinct and live a wonderful life in the matchless grace of God.

Chapter Three
Man: We Can get it Right

The basic instinct has become such an integral part of man's thinking and actions that rarely is thought given to it. We just naturally fall into the learned and conditioned habits of thinking that if we do good things then good things will result and if we do bad things then bad things will result. As we have seen in the observations of psychology and the direct teaching of the Word of God, this basic instinct is an inherit part of man in society. We have also noted that this is not a bad thing when man deals with man. Where would we be in our education system, the work place, marriage, or community if we did not strive for acceptance and reward by doing what is good or right? The problem comes when we bring that very human viewpoint thinking into God's divinely established grace plan for His children.

Our Education System

Our American education system has reinforced the basic instinct in the early grades since 1834. I use that date because that was the year the *McGuffey Readers* were first published. In Christian schools and education these are a favorite resource for teaching not only reading but also behavior and morality to children in grades 1 through 6. To date over 120 million copies of the *McGuffey Readers* have been published. In them you will find the basic instinct of man reinforced on almost every page. The *McGuffey Readers* are not the only materials used in schools that condition children in this basic instinct. Even the *Dick and Jane* stories teach that if you are good you will be rewarded and if you are bad you will be punished. Again, while this is good for training a child in how he or she should get along in life it does nothing to prepare a child for God's grace plan of salvation or grace plan for living the Christian life.

When a person is first confronted with the gift of eternal salvation based exclusively on the finished work of Christ on the Cross, the basic instinct will ask *what must I do? What work must I do to be saved?* Man is so conditioned to doing that it becomes difficult for him to accept a free gift. Our adding, however, of any of our work to salvation takes away from the work of Christ. Salvation is not 90% God and 10% us; it is not even 99.999% God and .001% us. Salvation is all in the work that Christ alone would do when He went to the Cross. All we can do is receive Him and His work by non-meritorious faith.

One Bible Question and Answer web site puts it this way:

> . . . salvation by works seems right in the eyes of man. One of man's basic desires is to be in control of his own destiny, and that includes his eternal destiny. Salvation by works appeals to man's pride and his desire to be in control. Being saved by works appeals to that desire far more than the idea of being saved by faith alone. Also, man has an inherent sense of justice . . . Our inherent sense of right and wrong demands that if we are to be saved, our *good works* must outweigh our *bad works*. Therefore, it is natural that when man creates a religion it would involve some type of salvation by works.[1]

The same web site goes on to say:

---

[1] https://www.gotquestions.org/salvation-by-works.html

The thought that man's good works could ever balance out his bad works is a totally unbiblical concept. Not only that, but the Bible also teaches that God's standard is nothing less than 100 percent perfection. If we stumble in keeping just one part of God's righteous law, we are as guilty as if we had broken all of it. Therefore, there is no way we could ever be saved if salvation truly were dependent on [our] works.[1]

As I think about my time in Liberia and the many answers I heard when I asked people how they knew they were going to heaven, most of the answers included some kind of good works or human effort. That is how we have been wired as human beings. Some of the answers I received were:

I keep the Ten Commandments.

I try to treat others well.

I do not sin that much.

I try to do more good deeds than bad deeds.

I live by the Golden Rule.

I go to Church.

---

[1] Ibid.

I do not cheat others.

I work for the government, but I am not corrupt.

I teach school but do not take bribes from my students.

Every answer reflected man's basic instinct. People may agree that Jesus died for their sins and salvation comes by faith, but they are so conditioned to doing that they must add to the finished work of Christ. They want some credit, some measure of doing, or some form of performance that they think will make them acceptable to God. In light of this we can understand why twice in the Book of Proverbs we are told (Proverbs 14:12 and 16:25) *There is a way which seems right to a man, But its end is the way of death.*

Grace: Always Free

Receiving something free or something for nothing is contrary to man's basic instinct. Man lives in this world having rejected the idea of the free. The acronym TANSTAAFL is common in our thinking; *There Ain't No Such Thing As A Free Lunch.* Others say that if something is free, there must be a catch, or it is of no value. Even President Theodore Roosevelt expressed this when he said: *Nothing in the world is worth having or worth doing unless it means effort, pain, difficulty . . .* In other words, there is nothing free. Mattie Ross, one of the characters in the John Wayne classic movie *True Grit,* has a line in which she says: *You must pay for everything in this world, one way and another. There is nothing free except the grace of God.* She got it right. In life the basic instinct works well. With God, however, it fails terribly. It fails because God is a God of grace and in grace we receive what we have not earned or deserved.

Some Christian faiths have a way of combining works with grace in a way that has man participating in receiving the grace of God. This is somewhat of a conundrum in that they admit grace is a free gift, undeserved and unmerited, yet man can do something to earn or receive grace. The Roman Catholic Church teaches that this is done through the sacraments. The official Catholic website states: *The sacraments are Christ's own gift that provides us with his grace. They are the divine helps which God gives us to enable us to: Believe the truths of his faith, Live according to his moral code, Grow in his gift of divine life.* The second one of these, *live according to his moral code,* has the person doing something, living according to a standard of works to receive grace. This combining of our works and God's grace is not peculiar to the Roman Church.

About twenty years ago a colleague asked me if I wanted to take a grace test. Thinking that I was about the most grace oriented person ever, I readily agreed. Here is the fill-in-the-blank-multiple-choice question he asked:

> God will bless me if I _____.

He then gave four possible answers:

    a. Do good works

    b. Show my emotional love for God

    c. Do Christian service

    d. Learn Bible Doctrine

Being a grace-oriented pastor, I quickly rejected the first three knowing that, while good and certainly a part of my relationship with God, they were results and not means of blessing. So, I chose answer *d. Learn Bible Doctrine.* After all, I had gone to seminary, earned a Ph.D. and spent my time as a pastor-teacher studying and teaching the Word of God. My friend then asked: *Why is number four any different than the other three?* Are not all of them something we are doing and then, in our doing, expecting God to bless us? If that is my final answer, then who is in charge, me or God? Just consider the common things Christians say about receiving blessing from God's grace. If I go to church, God will bless me. If I tithe, God will bless me. If I sing in the choir, God will bless me. If I teach Sunday School, God will bless me. If I serve others, God will bless me. If I am morally good, God will bless me. My friend then put the nail in the coffin of my works by asking me if God had ever blessed me when I knew, beyond any doubt, that there was nothing I was doing or thinking that deserved blessing. I had to say, more than once. He then gave me a new model:

> God says, I will bless you, trust Me.

That is what God wants from us. He wants us to trust in His Son for our Salvation and the deliverance from the penalty of sin and then to trust in the Holy Spirit for the deliverance from the power of sin. In John Chapter Six some of the more than 5,000 people who had enjoyed the miraculous feeding the day before followed Jesus to Capernaum. He walked on water to get there; they walked overland. They asked him in verse 28 . . . *What shall we do, so that we may work the works of God*? In their basic instinct they wanted to know what work they could do. The influence of the Pharisees certainly had conditioned their thinking. Jesus, perhaps disappointed them since they were seeking works, said in verse 29 . . . *This is the work of God, that you believe in Him whom He has sent.* That is the work we are to do to be saved, to be blessed. We are to believe, trust, the One He has sent. We are to have faith in Jesus for salvation and have faith in the Holy Spirit for living the Christian life.

Karma

Have you heard the saying: *What goes around comes around?* There are many variations of this axiom but they all reflect man's basic instinct. Some call this Karma. I think it is astonishing that this word and this idea has crept into the church. Part of Karma believes in reincarnation, and that part is pretty well rejected by Christians. There are, however, other aspects of Karma that have become a part of Christian thinking. Sammy Adebiyi, a Nigerian, is a youth pastor here in the US. In a Church Leaders column on churchleaders.com, he stated:

> . . . somewhere between then [his salvation] and now, Karma sneaked its way into my theology, and I fully bought into it. How do I know? Because every time something good happens to me, I expect bad because I'm not that good of a person . . . I think a part of it is because I have a hard time believing that God wants to give me good gifts. But I think the deeper issue is my subconscious subscription to 'Karma'. But if I'm good enough or do enough good, then I can expect and enjoy good. But If I'm not good enough or my bad outweighs my good, then I'm in trouble. Bad is coming.

Pastor Sammy's honesty certainly exhibits the problem we face with the basic instinct. Even Christians fall into the human view point trap of thinking that if they do good things then God will give them good things. But if they do bad things then God is just waiting to punish them. *What goes around comes around.*

One of the best evaluations of Karma versus Grace came from Paul David Hewson. You may not know who that is. He is better known as Bono, the Irish Rocker and humanitarian. In a *Christianity Today* article August 1, 2005, he said:

> It's a mind-blowing concept that the God who created the Universe might be looking for company, a real relationship with people, but the thing that keeps me on my knees is the difference between Grace and Karma ... You see, at the centre of all religions is the idea of Karma. And yet, along comes this idea called Grace. Grace defies reason and logic. Love interrupts the consequences of your actions, which in my case is very good news indeed, because I've done a lot of stupid stuff. I'd be in big trouble if Karma was going to finally be my judge. It [grace] doesn't excuse my mistakes, but I'm holding out for Grace. I'm holding out that Jesus took my sins onto the Cross because I know who I am, and I hope I don't have to depend on my own religiosity . . . The point of the death of Christ is that Christ took on the sins of the world so that what we put out did not come back to us, and that

our sinful nature does not reap the obvious death. That's the point. It should keep us humbled. It's not our own good works that get through the gates of heaven . . .

Whenever I have shared that quote in a lecture I always ask: *How come an Irish rock singer with a humanitarian heart gets it, and so many of our pastors do not?* Karma does not hold a candle to grace, yet we are wired for Karma and conditioned to think that we only deserve good when we do good. This is totally contrary to grace.

Bono was right in stating that at the centre of all religions is karma. Christianity is distinguished from the world's religions by the divine idea of grace. You can always spot a man-made religion by how it creates their god or gods in man's image. Since man is trapped in his basic instinct, any gods he comes up with will also have that basic instinct. Therefore, in religion man must do good works, perform sacraments, obey rules, follow traditions, or engage in certain sacrificial acts to please his gods and perhaps get to heaven, paradise, Nirvana, or be reborn as a better creature. But then there is Christianity which is not a religion at all but a personal relationship with the God of the universe. Our God is a God of love and grace. Our relationship with Him is through grace and faith. It is not dependant on what we do and for that I am very thankful.

Romans 12:1

Few passages of Scripture expose the man-made religions of the world as to what they truly are more than Romans 12:1. In that passage Paul wrote:

> I beseech you therefore, brethren, by the mercies of God, that ye present your bodies a living sacrifice, holy, acceptable unto God, which is your reasonable service.

Whenever a verse of Scripture begins with the word *therefore*, we have to take a look at previous context. Normally this is very easy to do, just read the prior verses. Here, however, the prior three chapters are parenthetical where Paul is answering probable questions on where the Jewish people fit into God's plan for the church. So, the context of Romans 12:1 really goes back to the end of Romans Chapter 8. The last verses of that great chapter tell us of our security in Christ. Romans 8:35-36 states:

> Who shall separate us from the love of Christ? Shall tribulation, or distress, or persecution, or famine, or nakedness, or peril, or sword? As it is written, For thy sake we are killed all the day long; we are accounted as sheep to be slaughter.

We see two things here that lead us into Romans 12:1. First, we are secure in Jesus Christ. Secondly, because we are in Christ we will encounter adversity in life. We are to present ourselves to God as a living and holy sacrifice.

There are four parts to this verse. First, we have the motivation of our sacrifice which is very important to our present study. Secondly, we have the conditions of our sacrifice. Thirdly, this is followed by the promise regarding our sacrifice and then fourthly, the reason for our sacrifice.

Leaving the first part, the motivation, for last, we see the two conditions of our sacrifice. The conditions of our sacrifice of self is that we are to present ourselves as a *living* and *holy* sacrifice. Our Lord Jesus had to give Himself as a dying sacrifice. Because of His death we can offer ourselves as a living sacrifice. We are also to sacrifice ourselves as holy. The only way we can be holy is not by our works but when we are walking in the Spirit by faith. This requires that we stop denying our sins and admit our sins (1 John 1:9) and turn by faith to the Holy Spirit to fill us (Ephesians 5:18).

The third part of the verse is a promise. God says that when we present ourselves as a living and holy sacrifice He will accept our sacrifice. This flies in the face of religion. In man's religions the worshipper is unsure if his sacrifice will be accepted by his god. We never have to worry about that. Our God is in the business of accepting those who come to Him by faith.

We then have the reason for this. In the final words of the verse Paul says that our sacrifice is *your reasonable service*. The word *reasonable* is the Greek word *logikos* from which we have our English word *logical*. So, doing this is logical in light of the context at the end of Romans Chapter 8. Because we are secure in Christ and because we face adversity, we need to be constantly presenting ourselves to God as a living and holy sacrifice. This makes sense for the child of God because God the Father will always accept the believer's sacrifice of self.

Going back to the first part of this verse we see the motivation Paul gives us for our sacrifice of self. It is by the means of and because of the *mercies of God*. We then sacrifice ourselves because we have already received the mercies of God, not to earn the mercies of God. This is what turns religion on its head. In every religion of the world and even with some false Christian teaching, we must offer sacrifices to receive blessings. That is not grace. In religion we not only are trying to earn mercy, grace, and blessing by doing something, but then the person is not even sure if his god or gods will accept his sacrifice. This is not so with the relationship we have with God through Christ and in the power of the Holy Spirit.

In man's basic instinct he wants to do something, offer some sacrifice that he first hopes his god will accept and then secondly hope that from it he will receive blessing.

That is the way religion works: man doing and expecting his god to bless him. Since man is making his god in his image, it understandable that this god would have the same basic instinct as man. But our faith is the opposite. God has already (Ephesians 1:3) *blessed us with every spiritual blessing in the heavenly places in Christ.* Therefore, our sacrifice, even our work, is not done to receive blessing but is done because we have already been blessed.

Even knowing that, however, our basic instinct is so conditioned in us, so much a part of our life, that we still want to do and do and do in hopes that God will bless us. Perhaps the most difficult task before the child of God is to set aside his basic instinct in living the Christian life.

Sowing and Reaping?

We have observed that there is a lot in the Bible, especially in the Book of Proverbs, that appeals to man's basic instinct. God revealed His word to the world but Satan loves chaos. He wants the world to run off the rails in hopes that he can pick up the pieces. God's divine institutions of freewill, marriage, family, and nationalism protect man and provide order on planet earth for everyone. God teaches even unbelieving man how to function within this order. This order functions within society by man's basic instinct. As mentioned previously, it is good for man to treat others well and to avoid lawlessness. Even as believers we still use our basic instinct in our dealings with others in the family, in school, in the workplace, and in society. We must not, however, try to use what works with our fellow man in our relationship with God who wants to give us His grace. Again (Isaiah 55:8) *My thoughts are not your thoughts, Nor are your ways My ways, declares the LORD.* So we must set our ways, our basic instinct, aside in our grace and faith relationship with God.

Whenever I have taught these truths there is someone who will object by bringing up Galatians 6:7 which states: *Do not be deceived, God is not mocked; for whatever a man sows, this he will also reap.* Taking this verse out of context ignores the next verse, especially the second part of the next verse. Galatians 6:8 states: *For the one who sows to his own flesh will from the flesh reap corruption, but the one who sows to the Spirit will from the Spirit reap eternal life.* What should we sow? Where should we sow? If we are sowing to the flesh, then nothing good will come from it. Instead, we are to sow, invest, plant into the Holy Spirit. What is the seed we have to sow? What is the only seed that we have that we can bring to the plowed fields of grace? Our only seed is faith.

I am very glad that in Christ I have not and do not reap what I have sown. Instead I reap what Jesus Christ sowed on the Cross for me. He sowed His life and from that unique once and for all sacrifice I reap the forgiveness of my sins, a personal relationship with Him, and eternal life. Our Lord also had something to say about sowing and reaping in Matthew 6:26:

> Look at the birds of the air, that they do not sow, nor reap nor gather into barns, and yet your heavenly Father feeds them. Are you not worth much more than they?

It is clear from Scripture that we are to depend upon God's grace by faith alone. Just as we were saved by grace through faith we can continue to live our lives in Christ through grace by faith. Paul said in Colossians 2:6, *Therefore as you have received Christ Jesus the Lord, so walk in Him.* We received the Lord by grace through faith and now we are to live before Him by grace through faith. To do this we must reject our basic instinct and receive the matchless grace of God.

When Did This all Begin?

When did this basic instinct enter into the thinking of the human race? As with all beginnings, we must go back to the book of beginnings, Genesis. In Genesis we will find that the basic instinct of man finds it source in the divine narratives of creation and the fall. In the Garden of Eden

Adam and the woman[1] enjoyed the grace of God. There was nothing to earn or deserve.

The Lord's fellowship with them was grace. God gave them everything. God even gave Adam the woman after Adam realized there was not (Genesis 2:20) *a helper suitable for him*. In the pristine and perfect environment of the garden there was only one prohibition. God said in Genesis 2:16-17 . . . *From any tree of the garden you may eat freely; but from the tree of the knowledge of good and evil you shall not eat, for in the day that you eat from it you will surely die.*

The name of the prohibited tree is very important. It is not as sometimes called *the tree of good and evil*. The Lord called it the tree of the *knowledge* of good and evil. What will be gained by the eating of the tree is knowledge. This is a knowledge that God did not want man to have. Some Bible teachers assume that this is a merism. That figure of speech sees two opposites being mentioned to imply everything in between. The Bible does include merisms. Phrases such as *heaven and hell, going out and coming in*, even *Alpha and Omega* are merisms. I think, however, that the tree of the knowledge of good and evil does not fit this figure of speech. Those who support this idea of a merism miss the fact that the emphasis is on the

---

[1] We often talk of Adam and Eve in the Garden, but the woman was not called Eve until after the Fall (Genesis 3:20). Prior to the fall she is referred to by Adam as *woman* as in Genesis 2:23.

knowledge of something that was not known in the perfect creation of the garden. In the garden Adam and the woman knew God and knew that which was good. More than ten times in the first two chapters of Genesis God declared something to be good. Man and woman had a knowledge of good because they had a personal knowledge of God Who is good.

Whatever knowledge the eating of this forbidden tree would bring was a knowledge that Adam and woman did not have prior to the fall. Truth can sometimes be found in some unusual places. Although we would not put much weight in what is taught by extreme Jewish mystical sects it is at least of novel interest to hear what they say about this passage. The mystical Jewish Zohar makes this claim about the tree of the knowledge of good and evil: *The tree of knowledge of good and evil, if they are rewarded – good, if they are not rewarded – bad.*[1] Although this writing turns around the idea of good and bad, reward and no reward, the basic teaching comes close to the truth. The tree of the knowledge of good and evil gave fallen man the knowledge that if he did good he would be rewarded and if he did evil he would be

---

[1] The Zohar is the foundational work in the literature of Jewish mystical thought known as *Kabbalah*. It is a group of books including commentary on the mystical aspects of the Torah and scriptural interpretations as well as material on mysticism, mythical cosmogony, and mystical psychology. Kabbalah is considered an apostate cult within Judaism.

punished. This was completely the opposite of *grace* which is neither earned or deserved.

Their new knowledge was well illustrated in what they did as soon as they fell. Their first act after the fall was not an act of sin but of good. They found themselves naked. They decided that was not good, so they made a decision to do something about it. What they did was good in their estimation and perhaps even in ours. They (Genesis 3:7) *sewed fig leaves together and made themselves loin coverings*. In their doing of good they determined that since everything was now okay between them it would be okay with God.[1] They had hoped that their doing of good would be accepted and perhaps even rewarded by God. But when God came into the garden they were hit with the reality that their good works would not be good enough.

We read in Genesis 3:8 that when, *They heard the sound of the LORD God walking in the garden in the cool of the day, and the man and his wife hid themselves from the presence of the LORD God among the trees of the garden.* When asked why they were hiding Adam said (Genesis 3:10) He said, *I heard the sound of You in the garden, and I was afraid because I was naked; so I hid myself.* What is interesting in

---

[1] There were three trees in the Garden. God's tree was the tree of life. Satan's tree was the tree of the knowledge of good and evil (the antithesis to grace), and man's tree of works was the fig tree were Adam and the woman got the leaves to cover themselves. This was the first act of human good.

this statement is that he was not naked. Adam was covered up with his new designer fig leaves. He, however, knew that in the presence of God this was not good enough and he was still naked. He still had enough of his pre-fall understanding of grace to know that his works did not work.

Following the cursing of the serpent and the earth,[1] the promise of the Seed, and a description of what fallen life will be like, God did something that was truly grace. We are told in Genesis 3:21 that, *The LORD God made garments of skin for Adam and his wife, and clothed them. God did this for them.* They did not earn or deserve these gifts. They did not participate in the preparation of the garments. These new garments were grace gifts from God, and it was God who clothed them. This is a picture of the slaughtered Lamb of God, His sacrifice for mankind, man's free will accepting of that gift, and redeemed man being wrapped in the righteousness of Christ. This is grace and by faith they put on the coats.

We begin to see the outworking of this new knowledge of good and evil, reward and punishment, in the human race in the very next chapter of Genesis. Soon Cain and Abel were born. We are not told how they determined to bring an offering to the Lord but they both did. Abel

---

[1] A careful reading of the passage shows that God did not curse man but rather cursed the earth and condemned man to toil in hard work to gain sustenance from the cursed earth.

brought a sacrifice from the firstlings of his flock to God. This was very similar to what will eventually be seen in the Levitical offerings that looked ahead to the sacrifice of Jesus Christ at the Cross. Abel's sacrifice was accepted. Cain brought a sacrifice from his garden. I have no doubt that it was a very nice fruit basket, but a fruit basket is not a picture of the blood atonement of Christ. His offering was rejected. We are then told that Cain became angry and his face fell. God even gave Cain an opportunity to correct the situation, but he did not take it. Cain expected his offering to be accepted. After all, he had done the best he could with what he had. He had done his best work. I am sure he was sincere and, yet he was wrong in what he offered. His basic instinct, however, gave him the idea that he was being poorly treated. He took his anger with God out on his brother. And Cain killed Abel.

Ever since the eating of the tree of the knowledge of good and evil, man has lived under his basic instinct. When man brings this basic instinct into his relationship with God it becomes his greatest hindrance to grace. We see in the Bible story after story of how man has expectations based on his doing of good things and not doing of bad things. He forgets that God's plan is a plan of grace.

One of the clearest examples of this is seen in the early life of David. During the time he was fleeing from Saul, he had become the protectorate of many of the landowners in Judah. These landowners provided a payment in the terms of supplies for David and his men in exchange for this protection. One landowner, named Nabal, decided not to pay for David's protection. When David learned of this he almost made the very big mistake of destroying all Nabal's family and farms. Had it not been for the intervention of Abigail, Nabal's wife, David would have surely done something so rash as to cause his own people to reject him. As David was working himself into a fit of a rage over Nabal's actions he said in 1 Samuel 25:21-22:

> Surely in vain I have guarded all that this man has in the wilderness, so that nothing was missed of all that belonged to him; and he has returned me evil for good. May God do so to the enemies of David, and more also, if by morning I leave as much as one male of any who belong to him.

Notice what David said, *he has returned me evil for good.* David was simply expressing his basic instinct. He thought that since he had done good to Nabal that Nabal should do, must do, good for him. Like many of us, David was living out of his basic instinct. Fortunately, Abigail was able to change David's mind and a possible disaster was averted.

The tree of the knowledge of good and evil may not physically be with us today but the effect of it still is part of our human nature. The knowledge of good and evil has formed in us our basic instinct. We are conditioned in it from childhood. It works in our relationship with others on this earth. But it is our greatest hindrance to our grace relationship with God. It is our inner enemy to Grace.

Whenever we begin to think that if we do good God must reward us and if we do bad God will punish us, we are going back to the garden. We, however, are not going back that that pristine pre-fall environment where we can enjoy the wonderful grace of God. Instead we are stopping at the tree of the knowledge of good and evil and, like our earthly parents, taking a bite. The basic instinct is an inherit part of us, but we need not let it be a part of our relationship with our Heavenly Father, through Christ, in the power of the Holy Spirit. That relationship is a relationship of grace.

Conclusion
What are We to Do?

I will never forget that Sunday in the Spring of 2014 as Pat and I, along with some of the other SIM missionaries, were driving back into Monrovia from our annual Spiritual Life Retreat. We had the local news on the car radio and that was the first time we heard the words *Ebola, Liberia, epidemic*. The reactions on the part of the missionaries varied. Some with small children immediately chose to leave the country. The medical missionaries started building the first Ebola containment unit at the ELWA hospital. We all prayed.

By April we believed our prayers had been answered because the Ebola threat seemed to abate at least in Liberia.

With that good news we decided to go ahead with our scheduled home leave back to the US. Back in the US in June of 2015, however, we received news that the Ebola virus had raised it deathly head again in Liberia. This time it was not in the rural areas but in the city of Monrovia.[1] We were planning to go back in early August but were told that only medical missionaries who did not have children with them were being allowed to return. We could only sit idly by and pray for our beloved Liberia. We were in exile in our country until early January of 2016.

The reason I share that story is because the Ebola epidemic in West Africa was spurred on by one very serious factor, denial. From the people in the cities to the tribal healers to the government medical officials, there was a denial that it was a life threatening and life taking

---

[1] There are many different accounts of how the outbreak in Monrovia started. One account I have heard from a few official sources was that a woman in Sierra Leone had gone to Guinea to care for her sister who was dying of Ebola. After the sister died she visited with friends in Monrovia and worked with them selling food on the street. After having contact with hundreds of people she too became sick. When she went to Redemption Hospital to treat for what she thought was malaria she passed the virus on to the doctors and nurses. The doctors and nurses at the hospital were stricken by Ebola and soon died. The woman died, her daughter died, her friends died and then hundreds, then thousands of others died.

disease This wide spread denial of the seriousness of the problem did not see official medical departments taking action until a month after the epidemic broke out in the city.[1] Pat and I were grieved to watch the news reports and see the dead in the streets and even seeing dead bodies outside our mission compound. When we finally returned we heard countless stories of how the government, people, neighborhoods, communities, and even some churches had denied the reality of Ebola. Even as people around them and close to them were dying many refused to face the reality of the threat. The denial of the seriousness of Ebola caused the deaths of many thousands of people in West Africa in 2014 and 2015. In a similar way, the denial of our basic instinct is causing the temporal spiritual death of many believers in the world today.

Denying the Problem

Denial is one of man's greatest problems, and the denial of man's basic instinct is perhaps our greatest problem to receiving the matchless grace that God has for us, not only in salvation but also in living the Christ centered life. Any recovery from any problem; spiritually, physically, mentally, or psychological, must begin with an admission of the problem. Jesus taught in Mark 2:17

---

[1] Initially Ebola claimed the lives of more than 80% of the people who contracted the virus.

. . . is not those who are healthy who need a physician, but those who are sick; I did not come to call the righteous, but sinners.

The irony of this statement is that our Lord said this to the religious leaders who were spiritually sick but denied their need for a Savior. Denial can keep a person from medical treatment and more so, from salvation. Many in the world today think they just do not need a savior because they are denying their sins.

In the same way many believers deny their basic instinct. They think that because of the works they do, living a moral life, going to church, trying to follow the golden rule, that everything is fine between them and God. God, however, wants the broken and contrite heart. He wants us to agree with Him regarding our depravity and sinful nature that opposes Him.

We need to admit that we carry in us a conditioned and reinforced way of thinking that is totally opposed to God's plan of grace. It is only then that we will seek the cure for our sickness. It does little good to admit that you are sick, whether it be cold or cancer, unless you take the next step of seeking proper medical help. In the same way, once unless you admit that you carry inside of your soul something that opposes grace you will never seek the proper spiritual help.

Finding a Cure

Since our basic instinct is the very opposite of grace the cure for it is grace. The basic instinct manifests itself in legalism. Jesus often used the curious statement that the *one who has ears to hear, let him hear* (Matthew 11:15, 13:9, Revelation 2 and 3, et al). In Mark Chapter Four He tells us a bit more about what this means. In Mark 4:24 He tells us to . . . *take care what you listen to. By your standard of measure, it will be measured to you; and more will be given you besides.* How do we listen to the Scriptures? What kind ears do we have on as we listen to the Word of God? What standard are we using? If you are not seeking grace as the cure, you will be listening with the ears of law and works. Everything you hear from the Word will be interpreted through the very human filter of the basic instinct. The result is going to be a reinforcement of your basic instinct and thinking that God is seeing behavior rather than your trust in Him by faith. If, however, you are listening with the ears of grace and faith, you will see the matchless and magnificent grace of God on every page of the Bible.

Just as you are told you should not mix certain medications that you are taking to make you well, you cannot mix grace and faith with law and works. Our basic instinct cannot be mix with grace. Essential to the cure to our basic instinct is to concentrate on grace. We do that as we come to examine God's Word and what He says about how He desires to bless us, to show us mercy, to give us grace. Paul taught in Romans 11: 6 regarding spiritual life that . . . *it is by grace, it is no longer on the basis of works, otherwise grace is no longer grace.* Paul well understood the power of God's grace. In 1 Corinthians 15:10 he declares that . . . *by the grace of God, I am what I am, and His grace toward me did not prove vain; but I labored even more than all of them, yet not I, but the grace of God with me.*

Living in Grace and Faith

Living in grace is like continuing to take our medications when we are sick. If you have a bacterial infection, it is not going to be cured by taking one antibiotic. You must stay on what the physicians call a regimen. As believers we must stay on a regimen of grace. This requires both a battle against something and a battle for something. We must battle against our basic instinct when it comes to our relationship with God. To be forewarned is to be forearmed. As we are made aware of the dangers that our basic instinct poises to grace, we need to consciously make decisions not to allow our human nature and basic instinct to enter into our grace relationship with God.

Our battle against our basic instinct, it is not easily won. We live in a fallen world among fallen men. In this world and those with whom we associate, work, and live, the expectation is for us to do good and not to do bad. We move, however, from the world's standards and expectations to a totally different realm in our grace relationship with the Lord. That is something we are constantly doing and often not doing well. Even in churches, where grace should abound, we too often allow the standards and thinking of the world to enter in and bring us under the bondage of legalism which is promoted by the basic instinct.

A man who visited our church told me that he was looking for church that had rules he could live with. He was blunt enough to say that but how many Christians think that same way as they search for a church? Also, how many churches identify themselves by some human and man-made set of rules? Often this is cloaked in what has come to be commonly called a *Covenant of Fellowship* printed on the inside front cover of the hymnal. What should be our Covenant of Fellowship? Paul stated it well in the concluding verse of his second letter to the Corinthian church (2 Corinthians 13:14) when he said, *The grace of the Lord Jesus Christ, and the love of God, and the fellowship of the Holy Spirit, be with you all.*

The Problem with Obedience

Often pastors teach that we are called to obedience as God's children. That, however, is only correct if we understand the biblical idea of obedience. The problem is that very few do. In the first chapter and the last chapter of Paul's letter to the Romans he bookends this great theological dissertation with statements that define what our obedience should be. In Romans 1:5 and 16:26 he uses the phrase *obedience of faith*.

Remember what we observed in John Chapter Six when Jesus answered those who had followed Him to Capernaum after the feeding of the 5,000. They asked (John 6:28) *What shall we do, so that we may work the works of God?* He told them something that we too need to hear. He said that the work His Heavenly Father wants from us is to (John 6:29) *believe in Him whom He has sent.* The Father sent the Son and by faith in Him we are saved. The Father also has sent the Holy Spirit (Isaiah 48:16, John 14:26 and 15:26) and we put our faith in Him to live the spiritual life by grace and truth.

Faith is defined for us in Hebrews 11:1 and commanded of us if our desire is to please God in Hebrew 11:6. Faith looks at assurance and hope in things we do not see. Another word for faith is *trust*. In what do we trust? There is no power in faith. The power of faith comes from where we place our faith. If you go out to start your car you turn a key in the ignition switch, hopefully, your car starts. It did so not because your faith was so great but because you put your faith in the battery and all the other parts that it takes to start the engine. All of us have experienced turning the key hearing nothing or at most a click, click, click. Was that because your faith was weak or because you put your faith or trust in a battery that was weak?

God had given to every member of the human race a measure of faith. Paul stated at the end of Romans 12:3, that *God has allotted to each a measure of faith.* The adjective *each* (εκαστος) is used as a pronoun and yet it has no antecedent in the sentence. When this is the case the Greek grammar demands that it be extended to largest possible number which, in this case, is the whole of mankind. God has given to every member of the human race a measure of faith.

We use faith hundreds, perhaps thousands, of times a day. From waking up to an alarm clock we are trusting is giving us the right time (at least more than twice a day) to brushing our teeth with toothpaste that we do not know its origin to eating food and stopping at red lights and going though green lights. But for eternal life we must put our faith only one place and that is in the person and work of Jesus Christ. Faith must precede obedience. If we do not trust God, believe Him that what He has for us and what He wants us to do is the very best for us we will eventually fail in our human effort of human obedience.

Many years ago, I was in a church in Southern California for a Wednesday night Bible Class. Nearly half the congregation was made up of what we would today call millennials. These young people in their late teens to early thirties listened to a message in which the pastor mentioned obedience repeatedly. Afterwards I went for coffee and desert with the pastor and asked him what kind of obedience he was teaching about. He very quickly answered that it must be an obedience of faith, and that comes from the Holy Spirit empowering us. I then asked him if he thought the many young people who were in his Bible Class that evening understood that. He thought about it then nodding his head, said that he agreed that they probably did not.

Since my own grace awakening I have felt that the whole worldly idea of obedience is being oversold in the church. If God just wanted us to be obedient and follow a set of rules, many of the people in cults and world religions would be far more approved by God than Christians. If we are honest, many Muslims and Mormons are far more obedient in their lifestyle and their worship of their god than Christians. But is that what God is looking for in His children?

My father was a southerner from Tennessee. He taught me to be honest. Many times, as an unbeliever I was commended by others for my honesty. As an unbeliever, however, the one who received the glory was my father. I would even say that my father taught me well and people would agree that I had a good father. When I became a Christian and started studying the Bible I learned that my Heavenly Father wanted me to be honest. When I learned that principle of truth I continued to be honest, but now my Heavenly Father received the glory.

Christian obedience means nothing if it comes from our own nature. The basic instinct has trained us to do good, but in that doing of good either we, or the ones who taught us those values, receives the glory. God wants us to do what we do not only because we are trusting Him and His Word but doing so from the power he provides. We do what God desires of us by the power He gives us. If we think that we can be obedient and please God in our strength or self-discipline, then what did God mean in Hebrews 11:6 where we read that . . . *without faith it is impossible to please Him.* Any obedience that we have must be an obedience that comes out of faith and must also be out of the power of the Holy Spirit who lives in us.

Back in the 1980s when I was the pastor of Hope Community Church in Arkansas, I developed a little formula that I believe helps us evaluate our obedience. It asks three simple questions.

What is your Motive?

What is your Influence?

What is your Power?

I called this the MIP for VIPs, very important people, God's people. How you answer those questions will determine if your obedience is of the flesh or of faith.

Our motive must be a response to grace. Remember that both believers and unbelievers are motivated by profit, pleasure, and avoidance of pain. Remember that God even uses these motivators with us. Here, however, is the higher motive that is only for God's children. We can be motivated by grace. Our influence must be the Word of God. We might be influenced to do good things by parents, teachers, or coaches but only when we are influence by the Word of God does God get the glory. Our power must be the power of the Holy Spirit. We have a choice of two sources of power, the flesh or the Spirit. When empowered by the Holy Spirit God receives the honor.

Only when those three come together is God glorified in our lives. Only then will others will see a testimony of God's grace, God's Word, and the Holy Spirit's power in our lives. Only then what we do will echo into eternity.

Awareness through Prayer

All that we have examined in this chapter must be initiated and accompanied by prayer. Prayer is one of the greatest things that we do by faith. As you pray you are speaking with someone you cannot see. You are speaking to someone you believe hears you as He hears the prayers of countless others all at the same time. Prayer, the very act of praying, takes faith. Then there is the faith and the rest that comes as you make your request known to God. We need to pray that God will make us aware of our basic instinct as it tries to intrude on our grace relationship with Him. We need to pray that He will open our eyes and ears to the message of grace that is found throughout His Word. We must pray that we will stay on the path of grace and not fall back into the bonds of legalism (Galatians 5:1) which is promoted by the basic instinct. We need to pray that our obedience is the obedience of faith and by the power of the Holy Spirit. We must pray that He will constantly remind us to check our motive, our influence, and the power in our lives.

Once we pray we must rest. The idea of resting in the Bible is most often the result of faith in God. God rested on the seventh day, not because He was tired but because His work of creation was finished. We too can rest because His work is finished. That is what Jesus proclaimed in His victory anthem on the Cross, (John

19:30) . . . *It is Finished!* When you are resting you are not working. You are by faith trusting God regarding where you are in your spiritual journey and what He has in store for you. Be assured that what He has for you is not because of your works, but because of His grace.

Five hundred years ago a young monk in Germany found grace in a world of works. His call for grace alone and faith alone were the sparks that ignited the Reformation. Martin Luther penned a devotion at that times that challenged the believer's dependence on works. The title of this devotion is, *Forget about Good Works:*

> Something inside of us strongly compels us to keep trying to earn God's approval. We look for good works in which we can place our trust, and which will bring us peace. We want to show God what we have done and say *See, I have done this or that, therefore you must give me your approval.*
>
> Each one of us carries in our heart a horrible religious fanatic. We would all like to be able to do something so spectacular that we could brag. *Look what I have done with all my prayers and good works. I have done enough for God today to be at peace.* This happens to me too after I have accomplished something in my ministry. I am much happier than if I hadn't done it. Being

happy isn't wrong in itself. But this joy is impure because it is not based on faith. It is the kind of happiness that make you confused. We need to guard then against the sin of arrogance.

So, we must not be confident in ourselves. We, who confess Christ, should always walk in fear and grow in faith. We should realize that we all carry in our hearts a horrible religious fanatic who will destroy our faith with the foolish delusion of good works.

The Holy Spirit provides us with a way to counter this godless delusion. We need to hold tight to what we have received through the undeserved kindness of God. God's approval doesn't come to us by what we do. Rather, it comes through the holiness of Christ who suffered for us and rose again from the dead.

In Acts Chapter Thirteen Paul and Barnabus were in the great synagogue of Pisidian Antioch preaching the Gospel of Jesus, the Gospel of grace. We are told in verse 43 that ... *when the meeting of the synagogue had broken up, many of the Jews and of the God-fearing proselytes followed Paul and Barnabas, who, speaking to them, were urging them to continue in the grace of God.* That same challenge continues for us today. My friends, I urge you to reject the basic instinct in your fellowship with the Lord and continue in the grace of God.

Epilogue

Are we on the verge of a revival? Christians have been praying for decades for a revival, especially in the United States. We often think of revival as many unbelievers coming to know Jesus Christ as their Savior. Perhaps the revival that is needed today is to see the many who are Christians, forsake empty traditionalism, legalism, works, religious performance, and ritualism. They need to awaken to grace.

We may be seeing the opening acts of such a revival. Remember in the introduction I wrote about the embracing of grace that Bart Millard, the lead singer of *MercyMe*, spoke of during their recent concert? I am hearing others talk more and more about their personal awakening to grace.

Perhaps this beginning of a grace revival can be heard in the lyrics of some of the popular Christian music that is being played today. Consider the message of this song.

> Some say don't give up and hope that your good is good enough, head down keep on working, if you can earn it you deserve it, some say push on through, after all it's the least you can do, but don't buy what they're selling, it couldn't be further from the truth.

Some say don't ask for help, God helps the ones who help themselves, so press on get it right, otherwise get left behind, some say He's keeping score, so try hard then try a little more, but hold up, if this is true, explain to me what the Cross is for?

What if I were the one to tell you, that the fight's already been won, well I think your day is about to get better, what if I were the one to tell you the work's already been done, it's not good news, it is the best news ever.

So won't you come, come all you weary and burdened, you heavy loaded and hurting, for all of you with nothing left, come and find rest.[1]

Maybe we need to stop and not just listen to the music, but listen to the words.

Pray for a GRACE REVIVAL

---

[1] Copyright ©, *Best News Ever*, words and music by *MercyMe*, David Garcia, Ben Glover, Solomon Olds. Universal Music Brentwood Publisher, 2017.

Printed in the USA
CPSIA information can be obtained
at www.ICGtesting.com
CBHW052011151024
15908CB00037B/670